THE TALE OF THE INSPIRED ROOTS

A TALE TOLD THROUGH 25 POEMS

BIJIT SINHA

ISBN 978-1-68494-223-7

Contents

Contents

Preface

A school is life at its nascent stage, always evolving, but never seen at its full maturity to the naked eye.

With each fulfilled potential, comes two more. And thus, the duty of the school to develop the youth is reset. That is the primary function of an institution: to let young life grow. An institution can never be self-serving. It shines because of the laurels brought forth by its fruit, i.e. the students.

But never does it solely take credit for the harvest. What operates in the background is always supposed to stay underneath—the true champions for its driving force.

When we began the exercise of writing poetry anthologies to celebrate the creative spirit of the school, I hoped to maintain a thematic connection between the proposed three. Two were already set in stone—one which explores the potential of developing talent (seed) and one which has assumed certain maturity (flower). However, with the third, we reached a dilemma—we could either explore another facet of the plant or we could take into account the reason behind its survival—the roots.

That was the catalyst behind this anthology—not just to celebrate the function of key educators as nurturing roots which dig deep to ensure the health of the plant, but to also amalgamate these disparate voices which could have been lost over time.

There is a common notion of teachers—that they are a candle supposed to melt itself while sharing the flame of knowledge.

However, what one often misses is that they can shine brighter and turn themselves into a young flame once again. What ensues is the cycle of learning.

For an educator can always begin learning and assume the role of a learner, wishing to breathe into a new life and propagating their knowledge until the end of time.

Acknowledgements

I thank Ms Vibha, Head of the School at The Ardee School, Gurugram, for her continual efforts to push the creative potential of the institution and let it evolve in a freeform manner.

I thank Ms Neera, Cambridge Head at The Ardee School, Gurugram, for encouraging the students to pursue their respective varied interests.

This project initially began as a CSR Project. However, with it taking a drastic turn and turning into a trilogy of poetry anthologies, I realize it couldn't have possibly reached fruition without the collaboration of the pre-primary, primary and secondary departments. It, after all, is the true testament to the latent potential of the institution as a whole.

I thank Mr Benolin who approached me on a dreary winter evening last fall, and proposed to take this trilogy forward.

To the educators from the past and present, you have left a deep impression on these students. Know this: you have made a world of difference to them.

To each of the parent(s), let this anthology be a celebration of the voices that are yet to grow.

To the teaching fraternity: we began as a family and we consistently put our best foot forward. Now, let us continue to nurture the young life further.

1. Vibha Gupta

Roots. Why do they matter?
Deep and invisible they go
Down the earth.
The beauty may have been seen
In the fruits and flowers.
But the base, its life
Has always been found in the roots.
The higher we will want to fly,
My friends-
And spread our wings far and wide-
The deeper we ought to be
Connected to our roots.

2. Neera Kanojia

Raising children with a rooted nature is a great responsibility.

Often touted are the ones below—

Honesty, compassion and accountability.

Every day, we attempt a new strategy

To strengthen those roots,

So the tender leaves can enjoy

What they have learnt about the world and its air.

The days when we succeed,

Are those when another leaf unfolds.

On those, when we don't,

We learn and try again.

Life indeed is a phenomenon

That circulates amongst these three things:

Learn, unlearn and re-learn again.

These roots are essential

To make us remember our beliefs,

And what we're worth.

With the generation of millennials on the rise,

I wonder if accepting change is the way forward,

If rushing onward with the wind is key.

However, acceptance must not come

At the cost of our own origin.

Maybe the way ahead is to make them believe,
Accept and reinstate faith in themselves.
It could be the only way
To save mankind, and in turn, ourselves.

3. Amrita Singh

Our world has turned upside down
Because of a deadly virus doing its rounds.
News and statistics of people perishing
Has crept too close for comfort.
We call it disconnect.
We are not grounded to the earth anymore.
Free to wander in times of extreme distress,
We happen to watch the world all over again.
The birds still keep chirping at the break of dawn.
It soothes our nerves for it is nature's alarm.
The sun and moon haven't changed positions.
Only the skyline with its shifting colours
Calls out for summer in the midst of a breeze.
We look for our regular working spots again
That have mysteriously vanished.
The tune of nature's music, although recurrent,
Is now falling on deaf ears.
Who would have thought we would miss our dreary holes?
Back then, it felt like we were working like machines,
As per the clockwork.
The joys of growing up in childhood,
With the tendrils occupied at work,

Are no more.
Instead, it is we who have to play the part
Of being a bearer.
It is we who have to lead the charge.
For change cannot happen
Without each of our efforts put forth at large.

4. Tavishi Gupta

I could not find myself
In this ever-rushing world.
I was lost
In the struggle of the corporate ladder.
Oh, I was so lost.
I'm burning the midnight oil
Soon to fade away.
Until the throbbing began,
As I shoved and they observed.
I jumped and they flew.
I spoke and they sang.
In their small world, I found myself.
I found my roots.
The roots that let me proclaim
To all of them:
Go fall.
Go rise.
Go lose.
Go win.
Go achieve.
Go create.
Go break every ceiling,

And live.

5. Ruchi Narula

When it's time for a flower to bloom,
It has to choose amongst several colours.
A range of seven from the rainbow
Just won't be enough.
In the darkness, it can't help but squirm,
Wishing for sunlight to arrive.
At least it won't be alone.
But was the flower by itself,
All this while?
The tendrils that kept it alive
Weren't the ones spreading in the still air,
But the ones buried deep into the ground.
Those that remain underground
Whisper for it to grow.
No, the flower was never alone.
After all, the roots have always
Been its true parents.
Maybe, someday,
When the flower recognizes
The reason for its survival
In the light,
It might just replicate the colour of the roots.

Not the grimy colour of the dirt,
But the original lustre before they
Vanished into the earth—
A pure, pearly white.

6. Atul Kumar Dhuria

Let's speak of a tale, often told in such a scenario—
A fireplace with the embers burning,
And drowsy faces wiped with interest.
A tale of the 'jaad'.
In other words:
'roots'.
Its importance often goes unsaid.
Why does it even exist?
One might ask.
It's gnarly; it may be the foundation,
But it always chooses to remain hidden.
However, the tendrils above---
The leaves, the flower and the stem,
Can't possibly let go of it.
After all, without it,
How would it even draw another breath?
You have, after all, taken birth,
From the roots of your parents.
You might stride alone today
With the lingering presence
Of the society's 'jaad'.
But know this:

Have faith in your roots,
For that belief itself
Will nurture you and
Cause you to move mountains.
But the sin of time running
May wrench the two apart.
I just have a prayer on my lips,
Directed towards the one
That resides upon the sky.
If there was an intent behind bringing you
To this world,
Through your 'jaad',
Why not take some pain
In making it smile again?

7. Rupa Rani Sinha

To my dear students:
When my eyes capture your presence
In those tiny window frames,
And as you settle in your spots,
And as your eyes return my gaze,
The sorrows that had plagued me
Begin to vanish.
Indeed, I have begun to forget my sorrows
When I see you each day.
I believe the companionship we share
Have contributed a whole lot
To me, my life
And reaffirm the journey I had chosen to undertake.
There are a couple of tenets that
I want to impart to you.
You may consider them words of wisdom,
Or words of introduction before
The real class begins.
You learn.
You grow.
You graduate.
You prosper and

You shine.
Soon, you will be a huge tree
Touching the sky.
Just remember, my prayers and blessings
Are strong enough
To reach you,
As you throttle towards the unending sky.
The pace of time is often noticeable
With the change in the colour of leaves.
Storms might encounter you on the way
Just to bend and twist you.
Remember what I taught you.
Remember you have to withstand them,
And remember I, the root, won't give in.
So, why would you?
Just remind yourself,
Your purpose is to lie amongst the stars.
Just remind yourself
This too shall pass away.

8. Shweta Khanna Raheja

When my roots turn out to be strong,
I can finally stand tall and proud.
Owing to my roots,
I was born with potential.
As a part of the crowd,
I learnt compassion and trust.
I can't just fly off with the dust now.
I was born with courage and dreams
Endowed to me by the Supreme.
My roots were strong, after all.
They kept me grounded and urged me to move along.
These were the roots that inspired me to grow within.
I may not have all now, but just enough
To consider it a blessing.
They won't let me break or bend.
They were strong enough to let me—
Extend above.

9. Rohitash Raj

While the world burns,
While people are at each other's necks,
All we are able to witness is war.
All we are able to live with is dissonance.
Often, we wish something could be done
To reform this world of ours.
"Peace be with you"
Is a phrase often shunned.
Selfish desires, evil motives and greedy hearts
Have kept humanity and mankind apart.
However, the root of this problem does not lie in one person.
Neither could a government be blamed.
All it takes to realise is a search within ourselves,
And a desire to claim the hearts of others and a 'conscience of
shame'.
O humanity, wake up.
Please wake up, before it's too late.
Let not the root of your hatred destroy this world.
Turn it all around, wipe it off your slate.
Let your roots evolve from a passion for love.
A love that is so bright
That it illuminates the whole world once again.

10. Akhil Arora

Most say that the expression of the first forms of art
Was born from pure passion.
But like the discarded carvings on musty caves,
We ignore the failures of the first of the men,
As they struggled to-
Find the right chalk,
The right rock
To embed and pass on their memories and their wishes
To us.
Dear ancestor, just like your masterpieces on rock
Were born from years of failures
And a burning agony to express,
We would like to believe we have inherited your will.
Just like the phoenix,
Our will to thrive has now been born
From the ashes of your longing.
Time has transformed the planet
And the way we have begun to live our lives.
However, one thing still stays true to our roots:
Our will to live and express
What we've always felt.
Why couldn't time change art?

Why did it never die?
Dear ancestor, the roots of art have only grown further.
Be it concepts, techniques,
Creativity or thought,
We are still the same cavemen as you once were,
Finding the right chalk to embed our emotions
On this world.
We think we have finally understood your wish now.
Let the legacy continue, you'd say.
And so we will.
Unburdened, we will transfer these four tenets of art
To the future beyond,
So that someday,
They too might think of us
As a memory,
As beautiful as yours.

11. Sakshi Sethi Arora

Igniting a curious flame
In the minds of the uninitiated:
Learning, they call this new phase.
The hands of the clock unwind
Into multiple evenings,
And the brain lethargically expands
In its most proficient manner,
As the lessons expand.
The work behind all of these
Does not go unnoticed.
The pages boast of great personalities
Who have achieved singular things
That might not be repeated in the course of history.
And yet, these lessons are rooted in encouragement
And nurturing love,
Hoping that these newer minds exposed to greatness
Could emulate them and take the place of the originals.
This entire process requires teaching—
A calling to mankind that has always borne the burden,
Often focused on spots beside the limelight.
And yet, without this unseen passion to inspire and lead,
The light wouldn't exist.

Without the reassurance of the ones hidden around,
The light wouldn't give its best.

• 19 •

12. Dheeraj Yadav

When the earth is graced with the knowledge of the sun,
It mimics its divine rays for the sake of its inhabitants.
For these inhabitants will bear the essence of light and learning,
Fulfilling the role of teachers who will strengthen the roots for the
future-
A future that is graced by the knowledge of the sun on earth.
These are the seeds that have been sown in the form of students,
Endowed with information above in the premises of the school.
The future seeks to claim them from the school itself,
Wishing for them to fill the shoes of Gandhi, Nehru and
Subhash Chandra.
If the foundation built is strong enough,
Our future will build the sky on this earth.
Enabled by the magnificence and a newfound affinity amongst
each other,
In ripples, they will spread the song of a new humanity.

13. Heena Madaan

Grandpa,
Your knowledge runs deeper than the roots
Of the tree you had sown,
On the eve of my birth.
You had said that I should always look up
And revere its grandiosity
And the expansiveness of nature.
You said that I'd always find my answers-
Rooted in humanity,
Always, in the form of spirituality.
But, Grandpa, wasn't that you?
You had protected us through all four seasons.
Just like the monsoon air slightly dipping the leaves
But never able to change their course;
Just like the sun peeping through the branches,
But never able to turn the matka water hot.
Those few rituals of yours in the morning-
Your words and gestures managed to warm us all
As one unit.
They often went unacknowledged,
Like the roots of that tree.
Both do bear signs of experience-

The wrinkles on your skin,
The warm presence you brought to the household.
On heated summer mornings,
Your words of wisdom
Acted as a refreshment to us
Fellow residents.
After all, Grandpa,
You are my origin
Since you gave purpose to my existence.
You gave me the strength
To seek out truth in the dense wood,
We call life.
On some days,
Your actions, silent,
Have become a testament to
How we ought to live our lives.
The leaves have turned yellower,
As we grew together.
But we haven't forgotten, Grandpa.
I have now begun to dream.
A dream to fly.
But I'm fully aware that this desire
Has come from the instructions of my roots.
Like a plant is incomplete without its foundation,
So am I without you.
Grandpa, your words have lived in me
All these years.

The everlasting nature of your presence
Has allowed me to stay anchored to the soil
And glorify the air that's about to come.

14. Ritushri Bangur

Digging further into the roots of the tree,
We find:
Those curled around love,
Those nestled upwards, hoping for the tree to last lifetimes,
Those that bind every single tendril together,
Standing watch like a guardian,
Those that have been nurtured with love
And watered with care
By their unseen benefactors.
They all embody the tree's hopes to dream
Of another new branch,
Another milestone to achieve in the season to come.
As time passes by,
Each day, each year,
We grow and bloom.
Little leaves and shoots are born
With the inherent desire birthed by their roots
And begin to embrace the sun and the moon.
The tree now stands tall,
As it faces the world,
Witnessing the expectations of man,
Having fully realized what its role is supposed to be

In this world of ours.
When this tree shall have an epiphany,
In times of bliss,
When the sun chooses to shine
With adequate amounts of dew,
It will remember.

Where it had started,
Where it had begun-
A transference of kindness
Born from the quenching of thirst
Of its roots.
The tree can finally see its benefactor now
As it prepares to give back
To those that gave it life.

15. Aashima Chaturvedi

A lonesome soul wandering through
The world seems endless and
Unbearable alone.
If only he had roots.

16. Rahoul Saigal

Down in the darkness
Roots connect us all-
The source of all of our love.
Stronger than an oak tree
Older than a bristlecone
These roots bind us all.

17. Shalini Panwar

We wear many different faces.
Some old, some new.
Some pretend, some true.
Some weak, some strong.
And some that just play along.
Some we agree with, some are just an adjustment.
Some make us feel empowered.
While others make us out to be a coward,
some are just a necessity.
And there are a few that just look pretty.
Some look common, while some look special.
Some are simple, while others present a riddle.
When it turns dark, all will be clear.
The whole world is asleep.
Thus, there is nothing to fear.
No pleasing to be done.
No room for pretensions.
Our raw thoughts, our one true face -
presents us.
How do we not think and reflect
and feel free?
Have we never wondered what we truly look like?

What could our one true face might have been -
Maybe an empty track devoid of a rat race.

18. Cherry Jain

Strong, sturdy or solid -
Be it a child or a plant,
A man or a tree,
Love, understanding and patience -
That's all you need:
To ensure your roots are secure
And hold you strong for life.

19. Bijit Sinha

Roots often lapse in our imagination-
as disgusting, spindly tentacles
that should be rather banished to the recesses
of the earth.
The earth which we often find ourselves in and celebrate,
but dare not embrace.
For we belong to the light,
and the roots-
away from us.
All we bear and desire are the fruits and flowers
that bloom with each season,
However, as they fall down to the ground
and turn squishy in death.
All we have is willful ignorance,
as our eyes are fixated on the bloom
that is yet to come.
We willfully forget
that we may join them in death.
Maybe then,
we may see them for what they are worth.
For instance-
if the roots chose to decay,

our eyes would forever long
for the flower that is yet to come
after spring.

20. Gurnoor Kaur Chhabra

As I was travelling through the winding path to Shimla,
My eyes greeted the lovely chinar trees-
Often claimed to be the rarest-
Their roots, hidden underneath,
Snaking deeper, justifying their magnificence in the
World above.
The concealed roots hold the tree
In times of leaden draught and flare,
Leaving me deeply lost
In the serenity of two elements in one entity-
One seen and the other
Working in the shadows.
My obscure roots could have been
My ancestors,
Who held me strongly,
Just like the roots of the tree.
Both in times of ecstasy and despair.
In a world of traps, we remain,
Seeking remembrance-
Of the fascinating world of these roots,
Far beneath the tree,
Deep beneath the ground.

21. Keisha Nair

As the petals unravel,
Revealing the ugly centre,
and the one below,
Hope seems to have faded away,
As everyone awaits their hero—
A hero who will walk across this piece of land
That no one can.
A hero that would save them all.
Little did they know he would never come.
Right here,
On no man's land,
Flowers used to bloom every year.
But now, all that is left
Is a naked centre bereft of roots.
Everyday, a petal floats in the air,
Acting as a messenger of the past,
Towards this land,
Landing softly on the barren ground
In an attempt to remind it of what it was before.
As the last petal floats to the ground,
The one that remains counts down the days—
Left in the dark, unmanned by the sun.

As he watches the last petal fall subtly to the ground,
He freezes and so does movement.
In his dreams, a flowerbed of sunflowers thrive again.
He opens his eyes and looks upward,
And the petal—
Refuses to fall.

22. Tanish Raj Jain

Our families are our roots.
When you're having bad times
And you're low and droopy,
They ensure to make you stronger
And give you strength and courage.
Roots hold you up
They don't let you fall.
After all, their purpose is to nourish and encourage you.
Our families are our roots.
They give us life and they feed our souls.
Strong roots make strong plants.
Strong families make strong people.
Strong roots lead to strong plants.
Strong plants have beautiful flowers
Who bloom and grow and flower into good individuals.
Therefore-
We need strong roots that support us and hold us up.

23. Kiyaara Luthra

Roots to grow and stand upon.
From the seed,
thus came a giant tree.
Now, it must bear the storm and heat,
and heal what's truly underneath.

24. Sidharth Bangur

There, on a hill,
Near a stream in the park
Stood a big tree -
Making its mark.
Part of its roots
Popped out of the ground.
They looked so great,
The way they twirled around.
Without the roots,
The tree would be dead on the ground.
And people would forget it like
It was never around.
The leaves would be brown.
And the flowers gone.
It would make you wonder
What went wrong.

25. Swati Sharma

I wonder what it means to have roots.
What they mean to me.
Is it just a word or does it -
Carry a meaning deep within?
Does it mean that I belong
Or does it mean that I go along?
Life feels like a journey
Which is sometimes light,
Sometimes bright.
Will having roots make me
Feel all right?
Sometimes,
I sit with a heavy heart,
Pining for a place
Which seems a world apart.
Will I find my place when I put down
my roots?
Reluctantly, I start looking for my boots.
There is a long way to go.
A long way to shine.
I take along with me
All that is mine.

In tears,
In fears,
In memories,
In smiles,
And all those paths will be mine.
Someday, I will have that root
That goes deep within even miles apart.

Authors' Bios

1. Ms Vibha Gupta is The Head of School at The Ardee School, Gurugram. An empathetic educator, she truly believes that the real progress of the world relies on maximizing the potential of students.

2. Ms Neera Kanojia is the Cambridge and Sports Head of The Ardee School, Gurugram. She insists on a compassionate attitude when it comes to learning.

3. Ms Amrita Singh is the Pre-Primary Head at The Ardee School, Gurugram. In her leisure time, she prefers to explore nature and capture its minute moments through her lens.

4. Ms Tavishi Gupta is the Humanities and Mathematics Mentor for secondary school at The Ardee School, Gurugram. She bears a secret desire to leaf through all texts of Indian mythology.

5. Ms Ruchi Narula is the ICT Mentor for secondary students at The Ardee School, Gurugram. She continues to display a caring attitude towards her students.

6. Mr Atul Kumar Dhuria was previously the Sports Coordinator at The Ardee School, Gurugram. He is always eager to include fun elements in his lessons.

7. Ms Rupa Rani Sinha is the Mathematics Mentor for primary school at The Ardee School, Gurugram. Always one for trying new approaches, she doesn't hesitate when it comes to incorporating new software in her lessons.

8. Ms Shweta Khanna Raheja is the Admissions Counsellor at The Ardee School, Gurugram. An eloquent speaker, she values

kindness at heart.

9. Mr Rohitash Raj has previously taught Science to the primary students at The Ardee School, Gurugram. An affable personality, he is considered the best of the teachers amongst the entire faculty.

10. Mr Akhil Arora has previously served as the Art Coordinator at The Ardee School, Gurugram. He has always championed creativity and its whims in regard to his subject.

11. Ms Sakshi Sethi Arora is the Pre-Primary Coordinator at The Ardee School, Gurugram. She has always been the favorite amongst the tiny tots in school.

12. Mr Dheeraj Yadav is the Mathematics Mentor for secondary school at The Ardee School, Gurugram. He holds true passion for the subject.

13. Ms Heena Madaan is the Science Mentor for secondary school at The Ardee School, Gurugram. She believes experimentation and a hands-on approach work best in aiding the learning of her students.

14. Ms Ritushri Bangur is the French Mentor at The Ardee School, Gurugram. A fluent speaker, she harbors an appreciation of foreign languages.

15. Ms Aashima Chaturvedi is the English Mentor for primary school at The Ardee School, Gurugram. She loves to regale her students with tales from the armed forces.

16. Mr Rahoul Saigal has previously served as the English Mentor for lower secondary at The Ardee School, Gurugram. He is famed for his attempts to teach the haiku form as a form of journal

entry.

17. Ms Shalini Panwar has previously served as the ICT and Computer Science Mentor for primary and lower secondary students at The Ardee School, Gurugram. With a penchant for creativity, she has always treasured the littlest expressions of the same from her students.

18. Ms Cherry Jain is currently working as an English Mentor for lower secondary at The Ardee School, Gurugram. No stranger to experimentation, she has devised unconventional ways to teach Shakespearean plays.

19. Mr Bijit Sinha has previously served as the English Coordinator at The Ardee School, Gurugram. He loves dabbling with folklore and turning them into fantasy adaptations.

20. Gurnoor Kaur Chhabra is an IGCSE student and currently pursuing Year 10 at The Ardee School, Gurugram. A good orator, she also has a flair for numbers.

21. Keisha Nair is currently a Year 8 student at The Ardee School, Gurugram. She has acquired well-deserved fame and is a national level player in swimming.

22. Tanish Raj Jain is a Year 8 student at The Ardee School, Gurugram. He is proficient at gaming and creating structures in Minecraft.

23. Kiyaara Luthra is currently a Year 5 student at The Ardee School, Gurugram. She loves experimenting with poetry forms, especially when it comes to creative writing.

24. Sidharth Bangur is a Year 5 student at The Ardee School, Gurugram. He harbors a deep passion for reading and has recently

begun reading literature centred on World War II.

25. Ms Swati Sharma has primarily served as the Hindi Mentor at The Ardee School, Gurugram. Another eloquent speaker, her bilingual proficiency comes to the fore when she translates certain lines from English to Hindi and vice-versa.

Printed by Libri Plureos GmbH in Hamburg,
Germany